Are You Speaking the Word?

Charles Cowan

Foreword

I've known Brother Charles Cowan since the Lord sent him to Tulsa to be a part of our charter class at RHEMA Bible Training Center. His consecration to the Lord was quite apparent from the start. And his fellow classmates elected him president of that first class. Now something else is quite apparent to me about Charles and his ministry, and that is a God-given anointing to teach the Word of God. His teaching sessions at our annual summer camp meeting in Tulsa and as a guest teacher at RBTC have indeed been blessings. I also hear of his personal ministry in the Kentucky and Tennessee area on a regular basis and then as he travels throughout the country teaching seminars and meetings. You know, there's such a thing as being a positive kind of proud — and I'm proud of Charles. I'm proud of his dedication to the Word of the living God.

Kenneth E. Hagin
President
Rhema Bible Training Center

Table of Contents

CHAPTER I

Contend for the Faith

JUDE 3-4:

*3 Beloved, when I gave all diligence to write unto you of the common salvation, it was needful for me to write unto you, and exhort you that ye should earnestly **contend for the faith** which was once delivered unto the saints.*

4 For there are certain men crept in unawares, who were before of old ordained to this condemnation, ungodly men, turning the grace of our God into lasciviousness, and denying the only Lord God, and our Lord Jesus Christ.

I was back in the children's Sunday school department of our church one Sunday morning, and I asked one of the little girls what she had learned in class that day.

"I learned faith," she answered.

"What is faith?" I asked her, and as she looked at me, I began to ask her more questions. She just kept on looking at me, not saying a word. At last, I began answering my own questions.

After I had answered two or three of them for her, she interrupted, "You catch on pretty fast, don't you?"

Well, I haven't caught on as fast as I would like to, but I thank God for what I have caught on to!

As I write, through the leading of the Holy Spirit, and as you read, may your spirit within you be quickened by the

Holy Spirit, and you too will "catch on pretty fast" in learning how to use *Rhema — the spoken Word —* in your life.

Let's read verse 3 of that small epistle of Jude again and see if we can "catch on" to what he is trying to tell us. "Beloved, when I gave all diligence to write unto you of the common salvation, it was needful for me to write unto you, and exhort you that ye should earnestly *contend for the faith* which was once delivered unto the saints." Jude is exhorting us to **"contend for the faith" of the gospel.** What does he mean?

The word "contend" in the Greek is EPAGONIZOMAI, and it means to *contend about a thing, as a combatant; to be intensive about maintaining something.* In other words, he is telling us to maintain the original faith of the gospel that was once delivered to the saints.

As we read verse 4 again we can tell that at the time of Jude's writing of his epistle the original faith of the gospel was being destroyed by false teaching. He tells us, "For there are certain men crept in unawares, who were before of old ordained to this condemnation, ungodly men, turning the grace of our God into lasciviousness, and denying the only Lord God, and our Lord Jesus Christ."

To whom was Jude writing? Whom was he instructing?

The first verse tells us, " : . . . *to them that are sanctified by God the Father, and preserved in Jesus Christ, and called,"* and he says in verse 3, **"Beloved. . . . "**

Jude was writing to the *dearly beloved.* And the "beloved" are the *children of God.* If you are a born-again Christian and if I am a born-again Christian, we are the children of God. We are *the beloved of God.*

Christian friend, he is instructing you and me to earnestly contend or maintain the original faith of the gospel that God had once delivered to the saints.

SOME QUESTIONS ASKED AND ANSWERED ABOUT FAITH —

There are many ideas floating around religious circles today about what faith is and about how faith operates. Some say (yes, even Spirit-filled Christians), "Well, sometimes faith works and sometimes it doesn't."

One night as I was preparing to go to church, I noticed two ladies parked in their car in front of my house. They sat there for quite some time. Since they gave no indication that they were going to come to my door I finished getting ready, and as I walked outside to get into my car, one of the ladies got out of her car and walked over to me and handed me a note. She was in tears, and she said that she was unable to talk. Just a few weeks prior to this I had counseled with her and another lady who was with her. I had counseled them in an area of faith: **how to believe God** and **how to stand in faith.**

That lady had a problem. She had waited until *Satan had* come in and literally *knocked her off her feet before she asked for help or tried to get her faith to work.* It was too late for that particular storm in her life.

Many Christians will wait until Satan gets them flat on their backs, and THEN they will look up and begin to call on God in the middle of the storm. They will resort to everything that they can think of. They will explore every avenue to get their faith to work. But it's too late then — in the midst of the storm. I am talking about that particular storm.

CONTEND? FOR WHAT? —

Jude tells us here that we should earnestly contend for it. Well, if you don't know what you are contending for, you won't know whether you are going to get it or not. You won't know when you get it. You won't know what it looks like. You won't know what it sounds like. And furthermore, you won't know whether you are asking in it or not — because you don't know what faith is (so many times). When I say "you" I am talking about the religious world and I am not pinpointing you as an individual; but if you fit that category, and if I fit that category, then I am talking to you and to myself. **We need to earnestly contend for FAITH.**

SOME ASPECTS OF FAITH —

Let's look at some of the aspects of faith. We will see if we can really put our finger on what FAITH looks like in one area. We are going to read a very familiar Scripture verse. I'm sure that every time the subject of faith is mentioned, this particular Scripture passage is quoted. "So then **faith** *cometh by hearing, and hearing by the* **word** *of God"* (Romans 10:17). It is certainly good to talk about God's Word. It is good to talk about this particular Scripture passage, but this verse says so much more to us that probably we haven't comprehended the full meaning of it. What is this verse saying to us?

ONE WORD, "WORD" —

Let's look at this verse in a little more detail. We will look at one word in particular as we read it again: "So then faith cometh by hearing, and hearing by the *word* of God." Now the word "word" is the Greek word "Rhema." R-H-E-M-A. If you go back and look at the definition of the word **"Rhema"** it will tell you that it is the **"spoken word."** There are two words that describe the Word of God. One is LOGOS, and one is RHEMA. *Logos is the entire or total volume of the Word of God*, and **Rhema is the spoken Word**, or bits and parts of the Logos that are spoken.

Did you get that?

I said, "Rhema is bits and parts of the entire volume of the Word of God: bits and parts of the Logos." For example, you lift words out of a sentence and say them, but you do not say the complete sentence. **Rhema is lifting bits and parts out of the total volume (Logos) and speaking them.**

ONLY HALF OF THE STORY —

This is where Christian people really miss the boat on faith. Let us read it again. "So then faith cometh by hearing, and hearing by the word of God." In other words, some Christian people today — yes, even full gospel Christians — think that all that is necessary is to come and listen to the Word of God. I do not minimize the importance of that, but that is only half of the story.

Faith comes by hearing, so first of all you can't have any faith in God if you don't know what God said to you, can you? You can't have faith for salvation if you don't know that it says in the Word of God that Jesus will save you if you believe on Him. You can't have faith beyond the knowledge that you have of God's Word. All right — after you hear the Word of God, after you know the will of God, after you have a revelation of what God really is to you and wants to do for you **or has done for you**, then the Scripture said, "Faith comes when you hear those things." In other words, "Faith comes when you hear that, and then hearing comes by the Rhema (the spoken Word) of God." Faith comes by hearing.

How do you hear the Word of God?

Well, you hear it taught, you hear it preached, maybe you read it, and you study it yourself. Maybe you have tapes or whatever. There are many different ways that you can hear the Word of God. But after you have heard the Word of God, then you have knowledge that God says that He meets all your needs according to His riches in glory by Christ Jesus, and then my Bible tells me that you are going to have to start saying something about it with your mouth.

Let's read that verse again and use the word "Rhema" where it says "word." "So then faith cometh by hearing, and **hearing by the** [RHEMA — the spoken Word) of God."

START SPEAKING THE WORD —

So many times people say, "I am not going to say anything. If God wants to do it He will just do it."

But He won't. There are some things that God does out of His mercy that you can't really put your finger on the reason why He does or doesn't do it, but for the most part God is just not going to do a lot of things for you until **you get geared up in the avenue of faith**. If it were true that faith comes by hearing only, then all that would be necessary for Christians to do would be for them to come or make themselves available to hear the Word of God and then faith would be in abundance in manifestations, would it not?

You and I both know that this is not true. *Faith is not in abundance in manifestations in the body of Christ.*

Why?

Because half of the Scripture verse that we have been studying has been left off. *" . . . and hearing by the [RHEMA —* **spoken Word**] *of God."*

CHAPTER II

What Happens When You Depart From God's Word

"Take heed, brethren, lest there be in any of you an evil heart of unbelief, in departing from the living God" (Hebrews 3:12). What does Paul call unbelief in the above Scripture verse?

He calls unbelief "evil."

FAITH-LESS-NESS —

Do you know a Christian who has said, "I will never depart from God. Not me! No! No! Not me! I will never depart from God. I love Him!"

After he said this, there came a time in his life when he needed to exercise faith for a certain need. And you ask that same Christian, "Brother, do you believe in God?"

"Why, you'd better believe that I believe in God. I will never depart from Him."

You may ask, "Well, do you believe your needs are met, NOW?"

"No — not now!"

You may make a statement like this . . . and if you do he will think you are "plumb crazy"! Do you know what "plumb crazy" means? It means that he will think that you have really "flipped your lid" when you ask, "Do you believe that you are already healed?"

He will look at you kind of funny and say, "Oh, NO! NOT ME!"

You ask, "How do you know you aren't healed?"

"Well, because I don't feel like it!"

"Hey, I thought that you said you would never depart from God."

"That's right; I will never depart from God."

Do you know, that Christian has already departed from God. Let's read that verse again and see what it is really saying. "Take heed, brethren [brethren, brethren, take heed, brethren], lest there be in any of you an evil heart of unbelief [that word "unbelief" means "faith-less-ness"], in departing from the living God." Now — watch this as we read John 1:1: "In the beginning was the Word, and the Word was with God, and the Word was God." What have you done when you say, "I know God said it, but it isn't so with me"?

There has just been found in you an evil heart of unbelief because you have departed from the living God. You have taken sides against His Word. "In the beginning was the *Word*, and the *Word* was with God, and the *Word* was God." Remember this: when you have departed from the WORD of God you have departed from God.

A THREE-LETTER WORD FOR "EVIL" —

All right, we read in Hebrews 3:12, "Take heed, brethren, lest there be in any of you an **evil** heart of unbelief. . . . " What little three-letter word would you call "evil"?

S-I-N, sin. Let's read the thirteenth verse of the same chapter: ***But exhort one another daily, while it is called To day; lest any of you be hardened through the deceitfulness of sin.*** Taking sides against the WORD of God will harden you, and you will be deceived in it. You will think that you are right with God. I hasten to say this — you are not lost. I didn't say that. I am not talking about being saved or lost. I am talking about operating in faith. I am talking about believing God for things for our existence down here.

"WHATSOEVER IS NOT OF FAITH IS SIN" —

Paul gives us a very plain Scripture verse in Romans, and I am not going to take anything away from it nor add anything to it. I am just going to read one portion of it, because I believe it is self-explanatory. "And he that doubteth is damned . . . for whatsoever is not of faith is sin" (Romans 14:23). Whatsoever is not of faith is what?

SIN.

It is amazing when we talk to people about what we call our "major sins," such as gambling, drinking, and all of those things that we call our "major sins." We will say, "I tell you, I wouldn't have a thing to do with that. That is really bad."
Well, you ought not to. But when we come down into an area called "FAITH," and the Word says, " . . . whatsoever is not of *faith* is *sin*," and it exhorts us, " . . . *lest there be in any of you an evil heart of unbelief, in departing from the living God,*" be careful lest you do depart from God's Word through faith-less-ness.

CHAPTER III

An Evil Report

As we talk about the Rhema of God, speaking the Word of God, let's see if we can see ourselves in the following Scripture passage. "And they went and came to Moses, and to Aaron, and to all the congregation of the children of Israel, unto the wilderness of Paran, to Kadesh; and brought back word unto them, and unto all the congregation, and shewed them the fruit of the land. And they told him, and said, We came unto the land whither thou sentest us, and surely it floweth with milk and honey; and this is the fruit of it. Nevertheless the people be strong that dwell in the land, and the cities are walled, and very great: and moreover we saw the children of Anak there. The Amalekites dwell in the land of the south: and the Hittites, and the Jebusites, and the Amorites, dwell in the mountains: and the Canaanites dwell by the sea, and by the coast of Jordan. And Caleb stilled the people before Moses, and said, Let us go up at once, and possess it; for we are well able to overcome it. But the men that went up with him said, We be not able to go up against the people; for they are stronger than we. And **they brought up an evil report of the land** which they had searched unto the children of Israel, saying, The land, through which we have gone to search it, is a land that eateth up the inhabitants thereof; and all the people that we saw in it are men of a great stature. And there we saw the giants, the sons of Anak, which come of the giants: and we were in our own sight as grasshoppers, and so we were in their sight" (Numbers 13:26-33).

THE MAJORITY WASN'T RIGHT —

In verse 30 of the above Scripture passage we read, "And Caleb stilled the people before Moses, and said. . . . " This is very important to you and to me. What was happening here?

Ten came back with an evil report, and two (Caleb and Joshua) came back with a good report. The ten said, "Surely the land is just like God said it was. It flows with milk and honey; NEVERTHELESS (nevertheless is just like saying "but" — "I know God said it, but . . . "), the people are strong that dwell in that land." Now watch this: they went on talking, and they talked, and talked, and talked. They gave a detailed description that the people were strong, the cities were walled, and they went on and told who was dwelling in the land, and by the sea, and by the coast of Jordan.

Suddenly Caleb came out there and said something like this: "Will you folks shut up!" Caleb didn't want to be smart, but he had a reason for doing that. Let us read it: "And Caleb stilled the people before Moses, and said, Let us go up at once, and possess it. . . . "

Now why did Caleb want to take the land immediately?

Because he knew and saw that **those people were operating in unbelief**. And he knew if he gave them two more days they would be back down in Egypt. They would not go to Canaan; they would go back to Egypt.

They weren't about to go over there in Canaan. "I don't care what God said. I know God said it, *but*. I'm *not* about to go over there. You can go if you want to, but I'm *not* going." That is what some of them must have been saying.

" . . . for we are well able to overcome it"! Glory to God. But the men refused to listen to Caleb.

"But the men that went up with him said, We be not able to go up against the people; for they are stronger than we."

And verse 32 said that **"they brought up an evil report."**

What does the Bible call evil in Hebrews 3:12? "Unbelief." The word "unbelief" means "faith-less-ness."

What were these people less on? **They were less on faith**, and you had better believe they were. They were less on faith because they **brought up an evil report** of the land which they had searched for the children of Israel. "That land eats up its inhabitants. There's giants there! We were just like grasshoppers in their sight, and in ours!" Even though God had told them, "I have given you the land of Canaan," they were bringing all of that junk and talking it.

Caleb stepped up and stilled the people before Moses. He said, "Let's go up and possess it now, for we are well able."

I can just see one of the older ones that had come up out of Egypt as he sat back there saying, "Now who does that little whippersnapper think he is? You just wait till he has been in it as long as I have. He's got a thing or two to learn."

I imagine Caleb did have a lot of things to learn, but one thing he did not lack was FAITH on this occasion.

When Caleb stepped up there and said that, some of those old saints said, "Well, Caleb, we know what God said; nevertheless, you don't understand. Those people down there are giants. Why, we are just grasshoppers in their sight. What do you think they'll do to us when we go in there to take that land? I ain't going."

A CHRISTIAN'S EVIL REPORT —

Many times Christians will want people to pray with them, to minister to them or something of that nature. They begin to minister along the lines of the Word of God (the ones who are doing the ministering). They talk like God talks from His Word and take the very positive approach that God has taken.

The first thing the one who has asked for prayer will do (in some cases) is to **bring up an evil report**. Now, I don't mean that they go to talking about somebody. They will say, "Now look, you don't understand what my specialist had to say about this. You don't understand the history on this thing. Why, nobody has ever been delivered of that; you don't understand."

That is an evil report of unbelief. The writer of the Hebrew letter called it "SIN." He said, "Whatsoever is not of faith is sin."

I'll tell you something, Christian friends: **those are the kind of sins for which we almost never ask forgiveness.**

Why?

Because we don't realize that we have sinned.

SIN BREAKS THE FELLOWSHIP —

Sin does not break the relationship with God, but it does break the fellowship. If we begin to talk doubt and unbelief, we are bringing up an evil report in the face of what God has said in His Word.

God said that you are more than a conqueror through the Lord Jesus Christ. (See Romans 8:37.)

God said that you can do all things through Christ who strengthens you. (See Philippians 4:13.)

God said that He meets your needs according to His riches in glory. (See Philippians 4:19.)

God said that by the stripes of Jesus you were healed. (See 1 Peter 2:24.)

God has made all of those wonderful provisions for us, but it is up to us whether we speak what the Word says and bring up a good report or whether we say things that are contrary to what God has said and bring up an evil report.

Faith comes by hearing and hearing by the Rhema, or the spoken Word, of God. You may feel like you have been run over by a truck, but if you are operating in faith you will say, "I know what Jesus did for me at Calvary. I know that Jesus took my infirmities and bore my sicknesses. I know that the joy of the Lord is my strength. I know the Lord is the strength of my life. I resist you, Devil, and you have to flee.''

To flee means to run as if in terror. That's what the devil has to do when you resist him in the name of Jesus.

Those people didn't get to go into the promised land at that time because the words of their mouths were not right. There was an evil heart of unbelief. And verse 32 said, ''And **they brought up an evil report of the land**. . . . ''

CHAPTER IV

No Kinks in Joshua's Hot Wire to Heaven

If you'll read the entire sixth chapter of the book of Joshua, you will see that the Lord had told Joshua that He had given Jericho into his hands. He gave Joshua complete instructions on how he was to take the city. And we read in the tenth verse of that same chapter where Joshua gave some explicit instructions to the children of Israel. "And Joshua had commanded the people, saying, Ye *shall not shout, nor make any noise with your voice, neither shall any word proceed out of your mouth,* until the day I bid you shout; then shall ye shout."

Why do you suppose that Joshua told them not to talk? That meant that they could not even say a word. In other words, Joshua said, "Don't you speak a word until I tell you that you can talk." They were not allowed to open their mouths.

If he had allowed them to talk, some of those Israelites would have gotten out there and the first thing they would have done, they would have been talking: "I don't believe we can do this. I don't believe it is going to work this way. I believe that young whippersnapper is off the mark a little bit. I just don't believe it is going to work this way. I know forty years ago it didn't work like that." The reason Joshua forbade them to speak anything was that he did not want any doubt coming out of their mouths.

Why?

Because doubt is unbelief, and unbelief is sin. Joshua did not want any sin coming in there because sin has a tendency to break fellowship with God. Sin has a tendency to put a kink in the hot wire to heaven. And Joshua didn't want any kinks in the line when it came to going up and taking Jericho. Therefore he told the folks to keep their mouths shut and speak when he told them that they could.

A WORD PICTURE OF UNBELIEF —

What does *unbelief* look like?

Let's turn to the Hebrew letter and see if we can get a word picture of what *unbelief* looks like. "Seeing therefore it remaineth that some must enter therein, and they to whom it was first preached entered not in because of unbelief" (Hebrews 4:6). What is *unbelief*? How was their *unbelief* working over there?

Their *unbelief* looked like this: "Hey folks, we can't take it. Those folks are too big. There are too many people over there. *We can't do it*. **We can't do it.** WE CAN'T DO IT." They were spouting that stuff out all over the place.

Finally, here came little Caleb along and stilled the people before Moses and said, "Let's get up there and take that land right away because we are well able to take it." Caleb's picture of faith looked like this: "Boy! we are more than a match for them. We are more than enough!"

YOU AND GOD ARE A MAJORITY —

Thank God! you and God are a majority. Old Caleb knew something. He knew that the great Elshadi God was on his side. He knew that God had said to him that the land of Canaan belonged to the children of Israel. Because of what he knew in his heart, he spoke that faith with his mouth, and he could not give a "hoot" what other folks thought about it. He just said, "Shut up and let us get up and take that land. We are more than a match for them." Although the "people majority" (ten Israelites against Caleb and Joshua) wasn't right, Caleb and Joshua, with God, were the real majority! They were right with God!

I'll tell you something, Christian friend; the Bible says that you are more than a match for the devil. It says that you are more than a conqueror. You have far exceeded Satan's ability and power. In fact, Jesus said, "Behold, I give unto you power to tread on serpents and scorpions, and over all the power of the enemy: and nothing shall by any means hurt you" (Luke 10:19). Jesus gave *us* the power to tread on the devil, to walk on him, and to put him under foot.

Most Christians don't realize that they have this power over the devil. Most of them say, "We can't do it. I know God said it, but . . . "

Read with me: "Let us therefore fear, lest, a promise being left us of entering into his rest, any of you should seem to come short of it" (Hebrews 4:1). We have taken that Scripture and preached that we have entered into the rest of salvation and that it is not by works or merits that we obtain salvation. But I'll tell you something, Christian friend; we have not entered into the complete rest of God that He has in His great plan of redemption that was consummated in the Lord Jesus Christ at Calvary. In order for you to enter into the total rest of redemption you have to enter into deliverance, healing, safety, and soundness. That's what the word "salvation" means — "deliverance, healing, safety, and soundness."

USE YOUR MIXER —

"For unto us was the gospel preached, as well as unto them: but the word preached did not profit them, not being mixed with faith in them that heard it" (Hebrews 4:2). Now, how would you mix the Word that you hear with faith? Remember, faith comes by hearing and hearing by the Rhema (spoken Word) of God. Where do you mix faith?

Faith comes from the heart, and your mouth is the mixer. Please notice this: if faith came by your just listening to the Word, we would all be spiritual giants. Caleb mixed faith with words and he said, "We are well able to take the land."

Verse 3 of the same chapter reads, "For we which have believed do enter into rest, as he said. . . . " What is His rest?

Salvation (deliverance, healing, safety, and soundness): we who have believed do enter into His rest.

How do you believe?

" . . . faith cometh by hearing, and hearing by the word of God." What does the word "word" mean?

RHEMA — the spoken Word of God.

This is where many Christians really miss it in the faith walk so many times: they have not entered into the total rest of salvation — that is deliverance, healing, safety, and soundness.

WATCH YOUR WORDS —

"For with God nothing shall be impossible" (Luke 1:37). We have all quoted that Scripture verse many times. We have testified to it, and we have shouted around it. Nevertheless, we have found things to be almost impossible. Yet we will quote, " . . . with God nothing shall be impossible."

Do you know what the word **"nothing"** means in the Greek?

It is the same word for **"Rhema"**! Here is how the verse reads in the Greek Interlinear New Testament: "Because with God every word will not be impossible." That means that every word God said will do what it says it will do. "Because with God every word will not be impossible." GOD'S WORD HAS POWER WITHIN ITSELF TO CAUSE

ITSELF TO COME TO PASS.

Faith comes by hearing, and hearing by the Rhema (the spoken Word) of God. Listen to your conversation and you will see what you believe in your heart and speak with your mouth. Are you speaking the Rhema of God?

CHAPTER V

Think and Speak On a Good Report

PHILIPPIANS 4:6-9:

6 *Be careful for nothing; but in every thing by prayer and supplication with thanksgiving let your requests be made known unto God.*

7 *And the peace of God, which passeth all understanding, shall keep your hearts and minds through Christ Jesus.*

8 *Finally, brethren, whatsoever things are true, whatsoever things are honest, whatsoever things are just, whatsoever things are pure, whatsoever things are lovely, whatsoever things are of good report; if there be any virtue, and if there be any praise, think on these things.*

9 *Those things, which ye have both learned, and received, and heard, and seen in me, do: and the God of peace shall be with you.*

What is true? What is honest? What is just? What is pure? What is lovely? What is a good report?

The answer, of course, is "the Word of God." Paul is telling us to think on the Word of God. "I can do all things through Christ who strengthens me" is a good report. It is in the Word of God.

The children of Israel did not enter into the promised land because they brought up an evil report. The Bible said, " . . . whatsoever things are of good report . . . those things

which ye have both learned, and received, and heard, and
seen in me, do: and the God of peace shall be with you."

Examine yourself as a Christian. What are you saying?
Paul instructed us to think on a good report. He instructed us
to think on things that are pure, things that are just, things
that are honest, and things that are lovely. But what are you
saying? Are you saying, "My goodness, if these prices get any
higher we are all going to starve out"? I have heard Christians say, "If things get any worse in the United States we are
going to have to go inside and lock our doors." If you do
this, you are thinking on an evil report.

A GOOD REPORT —

Here is a good report. "For he shall give his angels charge
over thee, to keep thee in all thy ways. They shall bear thee up
in their hands, lest thou dash thy foot against a stone"
(Psalm 91:11-12). Glory to God, let the world get evil — the
angels have been given charge over me and mine. Thank God,
I believe that.

I remember a story that was told to me about two young
men down in Dallas, Texas, who planned to burglarize a
home. They picked a home in a quiet neighborhood where all
the lights were off and no one seemed to be at home. They
went up on the porch and forced the door open, and just as
they opened that door, they stopped in their tracks. And in
the confession of one of the young men down at the police
station he said, "I saw the biggest man that I have ever seen
in my life standing in that door. He was taller than the door.
He was huge, and looked something like Mr. Clean."

All the pictures that we see of angels are little fat babies
with wings, flying around with a bow and arrow in their
hands. NOWHERE in the Bible does it say that an angel is a
little fat baby flying around with a bow and an arrow!

That angel scared those boys so badly that they ran down
to the police station and gave themselves up and told about

that *"big man"* standing there in the doorway. " . . . he shall give his angels charge over thee, to keep thee in all thy ways. They shall bear thee up in their hands, lest thou dash thy foot against a stone." Glory to God!

I was riding down the road one day with some of the kids in the car when I looked over in a field and saw some men trying to get a bulldozer up onto a truck. The thing had slipped off the side of the truck and it looked as if at any moment it was going to tilt. There was a Volkswagen in front of me, and when I turned back to my driving, the front of my car was almost upon that Volkswagen. My first reaction was to turn that wheel as fast as I could, but there was no way that I could miss plowing right into the back of that little car. The next thing that I realized, Christian friend, I was on the other side of the road, even with the Volkswagen and passing it!

Now — I know how I got there. I don't know whether you would concur with me or not, but I know what happened. My angels picked my car up and set me over on the other side of that road, lest I dash my foot against that Volkswagen. I believe that. If I believe God's Word, I have to believe that. AMEN.

JESUS DEFEATED THE DEVIL FOR US —

Jesus defeated the devil. Glory to God! "Forasmuch then as the children are partakers of flesh and blood, he also himself likewise took part of the same; that through death he might destroy him that had the power of death, that is, the devil" (Hebrews 2:14). He doesn't even leave us any room to guess who has the power of death: " . . . that is, the devil." Jesus defeated the devil and rendered him powerless. He has said, " . . . I give unto you power to tread on serpents and scorpions, and over all the power of the enemy: and nothing shall by any means hurt you." That is a good report. He wasn't just talking to Caleb and Joshua or Moses and the Israelite children. He was talking to the "beloved brethren."

And we are the "beloved brethren" in Christ Jesus. I am a saint of God washed in the blood of Jesus. I am made clean and pure through Jesus' blood, and He is talking to me.

I don't believe that there is a circumstance, I don't believe that there is a situation, I don't believe that there is a place out in front of me but what God and myself are not more than a match for it.

" . . . faith cometh by hearing, and hearing by the [Rhema — the spoken Word] of God."

Can you repeat what you hear?

Many times a wife will ask a husband to go to the store and buy some beans, potatoes, pepper, and salt. He will ask, "What did you say?"

She will tell him again, and he will go to the store but will come back with mushrooms, cabbage, soup, or something else, because he didn't really hear what his wife said. If you really hear what somebody says to you, you will be able to repeat or speak it.

" . . . faith cometh by hearing, and hearing by the [RHEMA — spoken Word] of God." If you really hear the Word of God you will be able to speak it. When you speak the Word (the Rhema) of God, you are going to think on a good report. An increase in your faith is an increase in your vocabulary.

Proverbs 30:32 says, "If thou hast done foolishly in lifting up thyself, or if thou hast thought evil [unbelief], lay thine hand upon thy mouth." I am really going to narrow it down and tell it like it is. When we think thoughts that are contrary to the Word of God and speak words that run contrary to what the Word of God says, we have just thought evil. We have brought up an evil report.

Don't say anything unless you can say words of faith. A minister once said that when he started walking in faith, he had to learn the "vocabulary of silence." We all have to learn the "vocabulary of silence" until we can begin to speak the words of faith.

"So then faith cometh by hearing, and hearing by the [RHEMA] of God."

Put your hand on your mouth and don't speak those words of doubt. Don't let an evil heart of unbelief be found in you in departing from the living God. Take your stand on the Word of God and STAND there while the sun is shining, and I will tell you something — the storms will be few and far between. I don't mean you won't have any, but they will be fewer and farther between.

Praise God!